# GEORGE WASHINGTON'S SOCKS

by
Elvira Woodruff

# Teacher Guide

Written by
Linda Herman

---

### Note

The Apple Paperbacks edition of the novel, © 1991 by Elvira Woodruff, was used to prepare this guide. The page references may differ in other editions. Novel ISBN: 0-590-44036-5

**Please note:** Parts of this novel deal with sensitive, mature issues. Please assess the appropriateness of this book for the age level and maturity of your students prior to reading and discussing it with them.

---

ISBN: 978-1-56137-086-3

**Copyright infringement is a violation of Federal Law.**

To order, contact your local school supply store, or—

Novel Units, Inc.
P.O. Box 97
Bulverde, TX 78163-0097

Web site: www.novelunits.com

# Table of Contents

# Skills and Strategies

### Comprehension
Creative thinking, identifying attributes, predicting, inferring, supporting judgments, cause/effect

### Writing
Creative writing, personal narrative, letter, poem, journalism

### Critical Thinking
Brainstorming, research, analysis, compare/contrast, fact/opinion

### Vocabulary
Definitions, target words, synonyms/antonyms, homophones, root words

### Listening/Speaking
Discussion, debate, dramatization, oral presentation

### Literary Elements
Characterization, setting, conflict, theme, dialogue, author's purpose, point of view

### Across the Curriculum
Social Studies—culture, history, Revolutionary War, recipes, currency, maps and geography; Science—time travel, moon phases, survival; Health—fire safety, frostbite; Music—drums; Art—design, time line, illustration, models

**Genre:** historical fiction; fantasy

**Setting:** present-day Rumson, Nebraska; 1776 Delaware River, New Jersey

**Point of View:** third person

**Themes:** war, courage, leadership, freedom, adventure, friendship, death

**Conflict:** person vs. nature, person vs. society, person vs. person, person vs. self

**Tone:** informational, sincere, humorous

**Date of First Publication:** 1991

## Summary

The Adventure Club's first camp-out turns into more of an adventure than Matt, Q, Hooter, Tony, and Katie had planned when a mysterious rowboat transports them back in time to 1776. They meet George Washington and the Continental Army crossing the Delaware River on the way to the Battle of Trenton. As leader of the Adventure Club, Matt takes responsibility for getting everyone home safely, but first they must survive freezing temperatures, a midnight march, Indian scouts, Hessian soldiers, and the horrors of war. They discover being involved in the Revolutionary War is a lot different than reading about the war in textbooks. Matt finds his own strength after witnessing Washington's leadership and the soldiers' courage—on both sides. Once they are safe at home, everyone realizes that living in his or her own time is best, though Matt hopes the other Adventure Club members will soon be ready for another time-travel adventure.

## About the Author

Elvira Woodruff was born and raised in New Jersey. She attended Adelphi University and then Boston University, majoring in English Literature, until she quit school at age 19—too restless to sit in a classroom. For 15 years, she held a variety of jobs, including janitor, gardener, ice-cream truck driver, window-dresser, and storyteller in a library, before becoming a writer with the guidance of her cousin, children's author and illustrator Frank Asch. Between writing, speaking in schools about creative writing, and traveling for research, Woodruff keeps her restlessness under control. She says, "This business of writing could never be boring because each story that I slip myself into is a new adventure." Woodruff has won awards and honors for her picture books and middle-grade novels. Her sons Noah and Jess illustrated her book *Dear Napoleon, I Know You're Dead, But....*

## Background Information

The battle at Trenton resulted in a monumental victory, a turning point in the American Revolution. The victory at Trenton, combined with the crossing of the Delaware River and the victory at Princeton nine days later, drastically improved American morale and provided new energy to the American cause. Soldiers who could have gone home at the end of December re-enlisted. The victory also erased any doubt in George Washington's leadership abilities and guaranteed his place in history.

The cover of *George Washington's Socks* is based on the famous painting *Washington Crossing the Delaware* by Emanuel Leutze. The German artist, known for combining political messages with his art, did not intend for the painting to be an accurate record of history, and historians fault his details. The flag should be the "Grand Union" flag or a regimental flag, not the Betsy Ross "Stars and Stripes" version, which didn't exist at the time of the Delaware crossing. Washington would not have risked standing in the boat depicted (as Katie discovers in *George Washington's Socks*); however, Washington, as well as his troops, would have no choice but to stand in the high-sided but seatless Durham boats used in the crossing (also not shown in the painting). The ice floe chunks resemble those of Germany's Rhine River, not the Delaware River. Also debated is whether the soldier carrying the flag is future President James Monroe, who was present at the crossing, and whether the black rower is Prince Whipple, an African-American slave who served in the Revolution. Washington is portrayed as older, more like he looked as President, than the middle-aged man he was in 1776. Despite the inaccuracies, *Washington Crossing the Delaware* became an iconic image, a patriotic symbol of an important event in the fight for American independence.

## Characters

**Matthew Carlton:** leader and president of the Adventure Club; participates in the march to Trenton and befriends Israel Gates
**Katie Carlton:** Matt's seven-year-old sister; rescued by George Washington
**Tony:** scout of the Adventure Club; short and cautious
**Q (Quentin):** brain of the Adventure Club; collects historical items
**Hooter (Brian Melrose):** muscle of the Adventure Club; sensitive, trusting
**Mr. and Mrs. Carlton:** Matt and Katie's parents
**Israel Gates:** rebel soldier; Matt's friend
**George Washington:** general and leader of the Continental Troops
**Nathan and Temperance Hornbee:** farmers; patriots
**Henry Schudder:** 13-year-old drummer
**Two Indian boys:** guides for the Adventure Club
**Gustav:** Hessian soldier
**Corporal Adam Hibbs:** grandson of Adam Hibbs, the missing friend of Tony's grandfather

## Initiating Activities

1. Prior Knowledge: Discuss with students what they know about George Washington. Have students record their responses in the "K" column of their KWL charts (see page 22 of this guide). As a class, complete the "W" column of the charts with what students would like to know about Washington from reading the novel and through additional research. The "L" column will be completed after reading the novel to record what students have learned.

2. Geography: Provide maps of the United States and New Jersey. Have students locate the 13 original colonies and the area shown on the map at the beginning of the novel.

3. History: Review the Revolutionary War Concept Map on page 23 of this guide. Students should complete the first activity, creating a time line of the events leading up to the war, and then discuss in class. Students can complete the other activities as part of the end-of-book assessment.

4. Predictions: Have students examine the jacket cover and then predict how the title will apply to the story. Students should begin the Prediction Chart on page 24 of this guide.

5. Science: Instruct students to research scientific theories on whether time travel is possible and what circumstances would be necessary for time travel to work. As a class, discuss how time travel might change history and the future. (See the NOVA program "Time Travel" at http://www.pbs.org/wgbh/nova/time [active at time of publication].)

6. Art: Have students create sock-shaped bookmarks (using cloth or paper) and decorate them with details about the Revolutionary War.

## Vocabulary Activities

1. Word Definitions: Have students copy a list of vocabulary words onto a piece of paper and write a definition for one word on the list. Students then change desks (their lists stay) and write a definition for another word on the next list. They continue changing desks and adding definitions until the lists are complete. Students return to their desks and write whether they agree with the definitions written on their original lists.

2. Vocabulary Chains: Assign a vocabulary word to each student. The student creates a vocabulary chain by writing the word, its definition, syllable division, part of speech, a synonym, and an antonym on different colored strips of construction paper (yellow for vocabulary words, blue for definitions, etc.). Have students combine their chains and display their collective chain in class.

3. Target Word Story: Instruct students to write an original short story using the following vocabulary words from *George Washington's Socks*: rebel, eerie, conceal, wriggling, terrain, adventurous, lush.

4. Homophones: List the following homophones from the novel on the bulletin board. For each word, instruct students to write a sentence for each word that shows the different meanings of each homophone: peas/piece/peace, weather/whether, blew/blue, side/sighed, bear/bare, feet/feat, road/rode/rowed.

# Chapters One–Three

Matt can't wait to get to the first meeting of the Adventure Club even though he has to bring his little sister Katie. At club meetings, Matt and his friends—Tony, Hooter, and Q—read about real adventures from *Great Adventures in History*. The first night's adventure is about George Washington's troops crossing the Delaware River. At the camp-out in Tony's backyard, Katie embarrasses the boys, asking when the adventure starts. Matt decides the club should have adventures as well as read about them. He talks the club members into a night hike through the woods to the lake.

| Vocabulary |
| --- |
| stole |
| suppress |
| desperate |
| smugly |
| rebel |
| bayonet |
| defeat |
| verge |
| abnormal |
| muster |
| charter |
| adventurous |
| array |
| arsenal |

## Discussion Questions

1. What is the purpose of the Adventure Club? Would you like to join a similar club? (*to read and talk about real adventures that people had throughout history; Answers will vary.*)

2. Why does Matt invite Katie to the camp-out? (*so Katie won't tell their parents that Matt hid his peas in the sugar bowl*)

3. Why is Hooter confused when Matt starts reading? (*Hooter knows Americans won the War for Independence, so it doesn't make sense to him when Matt reads about the losses suffered by the rebel army and how the American cause was almost lost.*)

4. Why does Matt say the crossing of the Delaware River is an incredible adventure? What obstacles did George Washington face? (*With the American Army "on the verge of collapse" [p. 7], the crossing of the Delaware and triumph at Trenton provides a victory that turns the tide in America's favor; food and supply shortages, divided loyalties, spies, ill-trained and inexperienced soldiers, and the harshest winter weather*)

5. Who are the members of the Adventure Club? Explain each member's job and why he is assigned that job. (*Matt, president because starting the club was his idea; Tony, scout because he is small enough to check things out without being seen; Q, the brain because he has "the fastest brain in the fifth grade" [p. 9]; Hooter, strong man because he is big; Hooter is also in charge of any stray baby animals because of his soft heart.*)

6. Why is Katie disappointed with the club? Why does this embarrass the boys? (*Katie thought they would be going on an adventure. The boys realize camping in Tony's backyard isn't adventurous.*)

7. Where did the Adventure Club first plan to camp out? Why did they choose this place? Do you think Katie would be disappointed with the club if parents had not changed the original plans? (*along the lake; to be like Washington and his troops along the Delaware River; Answers will vary.*)

8. Review how each character responds to Matt's suggestion of a night hike to the lake. Which character's response is most like what yours would be? (*Answers will vary.*)

9. **Prediction:** How will Katie cause trouble for the boys?

## Supplementary Activities

1. Literary Analysis: Begin the Story Map on page 25 of this guide. Add to the map as you read the novel.

2. Brainstorming: Write "Leadership Characteristics" in the center of a poster board. As a class, list characteristics and motivation needed to be a leader. Display the poster in class for the duration of the novel.

3. Creative Writing: On page two of the novel, Matt says he would rather face a bloodthirsty vampire or a wild cat than eat peas. Write a poem titled "An Adventure in Eating" about a situation that is preferble to eating a dreaded food.

4. Health: Tony's dad lectures the Adventure Club on fire safety. Create a fire preparedness video. Show how to avoid fires and what to do during a fire.

## Chapters Four–Six

Walking through the woods, Tony tells the Adventure Club about the legend of Lake Levart, where Tony's grandfather saw his boyhood friend Adam Hibbs vanish. Since then, Tony's grandfather has investigated other disappearances and heard fantastic stories told by people who have returned. Each had gone onto the lake in a mysterious rowboat when there was a three-quarter moon. The children notice that such a moon hangs over them as they walk through the woods. The boys lose Katie only to find her climbing into an old rowboat. Matt knows he should run away, but he and the others are drawn to the boat. When they join Katie, the boat moves into the lake and mist envelops them. Suddenly the Adventure Club is on a roaring river surrounded by ice. The Adventure Club is terrified when Katie falls overboard. They find an inscription in the boat that reads "Emit Levart."

| Vocabulary |
| --- |
| legend |
| fantastic |
| canteen |
| batty |
| comrades |
| eerie |
| transfixed |
| hoisting |
| vessel |
| mistrust |
| trance |
| feeble |
| veered |
| abrupt |
| floes |
| paralyzed |
| console |

### Discussion Questions

1. What is the legend of the lake? How does it change some people? (*People disappear after going out on a rowboat when there is a three-quarter moon. People who disappear and return aren't the same; they tell fantastic stories and sit and stare at the lake.*)

2. Why is Tony's grandfather interested in the legend of the lake? How many mysterious disappearances has he investigated in 50 years? (*When he was a boy, Grandpa saw his friend Adam Hibbs disappear on the lake; five after Adam*)

3. Why do Matt and Q both think losing Katie is their own fault? Whose fault do you think it is? (*Matt thinks he shouldn't have let go of Katie's hand, and as president of the club, he shouldn't have let Katie come along. Q says Katie put her marshmallows down to help him. Answers will vary but could include whether Katie is old enough to know better than to leave the boys.*)

4. What does Matt feel when he nears the rowboat? (*Matt feels wonder and terror; he knows the boat is powerful and dangerous, yet he is drawn to it. He also feels a strong sense of responsibility to rescue his sister.*)

5. What happens when the Adventure Club members board the rowboat? What is different after the boat's spell is broken? (*Their fear leaves them, and they smile. The boat trembles, and a mist envelops them. The lake is now a roaring river with ice, and it is very cold.*)

6. Why is Matt "paralyzed with fear and grief" (p. 31)? Are you surprised by who comforts him? (*Katie falls overboard. Answers will vary. Suggestion: Hooter comforting Matt should be expected because Hooter cares for others, both people and animals.*)

7. Which characters show bravery in Chapters Four through Six? Use details from the book to support your answers. (*Answers will vary but should include that all characters show bravery. Katie brandishes her "weapons" when threatened, and she isn't afraid to wander off by herself. In the woods, Tony scouts even though he is afraid. Everyone tries to stop Katie from climbing into the rowboat. Matt and Hooter try to prevent Katie from falling overboard. Matt is willing to jump into freezing water to rescue his sister.*)

8. **Prediction:** How will the boys find Katie?

## Supplementary Activities

1. Creative Writing: Write a story about how the legend of Lake Levart began. Write about the first person that disappears on the lake.

2. Science: Create a poster showing the phases of the moon. Include a brief report explaining why the moon's appearance changes. Use the terms "waxing" and "waning" in your report.

3. Comprehension: During the adventure, Katie falls out of the rowboat. Rewrite the scene with Katie as the narrator.

4. Literary Analysis: Choose a sentence or two of dialogue from Chapters Four through Six. Determine the purpose of the dialogue, telling whether it advances the plot, describes a character, or gives information to the reader.

# Chapters Seven–Nine

When General George Washington pulls Katie from an ice floe to the safety of his boat, the Adventure Club realizes they've gone back in time. They are in the middle of Washington's crossing of the Delaware River, and it's more of an adventure than they originally wanted. Corporal Adam Hibbs is assigned to take them to an inn. Matt wants to ask Adam if he is the friend of Tony's grandfather, but decides he must first return Washington's cape, which is wrapped around Katie. A captain takes the cape and hands Matt a musket. Matt's daydreams are suddenly a reality; he is a rebel soldier in the Revolutionary War.

| Vocabulary |
| --- |
| imposing |
| foe |
| muskets |
| foreign |
| perplexed |
| enlist |
| riveted |
| venture |
| resist |
| disembark |
| guardian |
| diverted |
| ensured |
| capacity |
| regiment |
| conceal |
| befell |

## Discussion Questions

1. What clues in the story show that the Adventure Club has gone back in time? (*the language and uniforms of the men in the boat, names such as Continental Army and George Washington, Washington's unfamiliarity with Nebraska; Answers will vary.*)

2. How does Matt describe George Washington? Do you see these characteristics when you look at a picture of Washington? (*"tall imposing figure in a blue and buff uniform...white hair rolled on the sides, and tied in the back with a ribbon...strong and proud" [p. 35]; Answers will vary.*)

3. Matt thinks Washington stares at him "as if one commander had recognized another" (p. 35). Do you think Washington sees Matt as a commander? (*Answers will vary.*)

4. Why is Washington disgusted at the thought of Matt and his friends being runners for the British? (*Washington thinks it cowardly and cold-hearted to send children as spies during a terrible storm.*)

5. Who are John Glover's Marbleheaders? Why does Washington owe them thanks? (*seafaring men led by Colonel John Glover of Marblehead, Massachusetts, who ferry Washington's troops across the Delaware River; Washington's troops could not have crossed without the Marbleheaders' navigational skills.*)

6. What is Washington's battle plan? How is surprise important to his plan? (*After crossing the Delaware, they will march nine miles to Trenton and attack the Hessians. The German soldiers will be sleeping after Christmas celebrations and won't be expecting an attack.*)

7. Why does Matt feel cowardly dressed in sneakers and a down vest? (*The soldiers are poorly clad, some without coats, hats, or shoes, yet they bravely march in the blistering cold weather.*)

8. Do you think Corporal Adam Hibbs is the friend of Tony's grandfather? Use details from the book to support your answer. (*Answers will vary. Suggestions: Matt is certain it is the same man because the corporal looked at him knowingly. Yet, Adam looks like a young man. Either time-travelers do not age, or this man is too young to be the friend of Tony's grandfather.*)

9. Why do the soldiers' uniforms surprise Matt? (*Matt imagined fine blue and white uniforms, but the soldiers' clothes are tattered. Many soldiers aren't wearing overcoats, hats, or shoes. Each regiment wears a different uniform and in a variety of colors.*)

10. What happens that makes Matt feel like a "true rebel"? What happens to make Matt realize he is not a rebel? (*Matt is given the responsibility of returning Washington's cape. He is handed a musket and expected to march with the soldiers.*)

11. **Prediction:** Will Matt fight the Hessians?

## Supplementary Activities

1. Art: Create a diorama of the Continental Army crossing the Delaware River. Use details from page 42 of the book.

2. Writing: After crossing the river, the soldiers march nine miles to Trenton. Locate a destination nine miles from your school. Write a one-page report about the obstacles you would have to face on your own nine-mile trek if you had cloth wrapped around your feet instead of shoes.

3. Social Studies: Research the different types of uniforms worn by American soldiers. Draw pictures of several.

4. Speaking: On page 48, some soldiers wear headbands with the words "Liberty or Death." Research Patrick Henry's "Give me liberty, or give me death!" speech. Have a class competition to see if anyone can memorize and recite the entire speech. Patrick Henry's famous speech is available online at http://www.historyplace.com/speeches/henry.htm (active at time of publication).

## Chapters Ten–Twelve

Matt is freezing and not sure if he can walk nine miles in a storm, yet he doesn't want to be taken for a spy or a coward. He feels safer when he makes friends with Israel Gates, a young, injured soldier. Matt is surprised when Israel explains that he isn't in the army for patriotic reasons; he's earning money to support his family. As General Washington, Colonel Knox, and others make battle plans, Israel realizes they will be fighting the Hessians in Trenton. He and a nearby drummer tell Matt that the Hessians are bloodthirsty giants. Matt knows the Americans win the battle with only a few casualties, yet he's terrified he could be one of those casualties.

| Vocabulary |
| --- |
| pry |
| haggard |
| vexed |
| ornate |
| scow |
| artillery |
| patriot |
| siege |
| expedite |
| chided |
| chapped |
| instill |
| scourge |
| rations |
| mature |

### Discussion Questions

1. What differences does Matt see between himself and Israel? (*Answers may vary, but Matt realizes how luxurious his life is since he can refuse to wear a sock because it has stripes. He wonders if he has Israel's courage to keep going.*)

2. Why won't Israel re-enlist in the army? Why will other soldiers? (*Israel has seen too much hardship and has had enough of army life. His regiment has been through a lot: pox, battling Indians in Montreal, marches to Albany then Pennsylvania. Answers will vary. Suggestions: Spirits are high because the army is on the offense at last. [The victory at Trenton followed nine days later by the victory in Princeton resulted in reenlistments.]*)

3. What difficult choice does Matt think soldiers make? What is Israel's response? (*Soldiers must choose between their families and their country, though fighting for their country also keeps their families safe. Israel doesn't think the war is necessary. He became a soldier only to earn money for his family.*)

4. What is the only thing Israel has to sell? What did he get in exchange? (*himself; Israel enlisted in place of a wealthy silversmith; in exchange he received a cow and money to feed his sister and brothers.*)

5. How does Israel comfort Matt? What do you think would happen if he hadn't made friends with Israel? (*Answers will vary. Suggestions: Not being alone and seeing Israel's courage keeps Matt going, and Israel might be able to protect Matt in battle. Matt would be even more frightened.*)

6. Why don't many shopkeepers "believe the Continental currency is worth anything" (p. 61)? (*Answers will vary. Suggestions: Continental currency is printed on paper, rather than made from gold or silver. People don't think the American Revolution will be successful, in which case the paper money would be worthless.*)

7. Matt is glad he did his report so he knows where he is and what is happening. How would the story be different if Matt had not done his homework? How would it be the same? (*Answers will vary. Suggestions: Matt wouldn't know that the battle results in a victory for Washington. He would still be afraid, not knowing if he can survive the march or the battle.*)

8. Who is Henry Knox? Why is he important to Washington? (*a Boston bookstore owner who was given command of the Continental Artillery Regiment because of his intelligence, strength, and patriotism. Washington is depending on 18 guns for the attack on Trenton.*)

9. How does the storm work for and against Washington and his troops? Why does Washington say their destiny will be decided at the battle of Trenton? (*The storm is slowing the troops so they won't arrive before daybreak; yet, the day will be relatively dark, making it easier to surprise the Hessians. Washington knows how important victory is—that if they are defeated, then Philadelphia will be lost.*)

10. Why do drummers wear uniforms that are the reversed colors of their regiment? Why is this important? (*to make it easier for officers to find drummers during battle; Drummers send signals from officers to the soldiers.*)

11. **Prediction:** Will Israel and Matt make it to Trenton?

## Supplementary Activities

1. Creative Writing: Imagine you are Israel Gates. Write a letter to Abby telling her about Matt and his strange clothes. Explain why you want to help Matt.

2. Health: Design a safety poster about how to avoid frostbite. Include information on how to treat frostbite. Display the poster in the classroom.

3. History: Israel explains that drummers give signals in battle. Drummers also signal soldiers about when to wake up, when to eat, when to line up, and more. Research other methods armies used to send signals to their troops, and create a poster or write a report detailing your findings.

# Chapters Thirteen–Fifteen

When Israel collapses, Henry encourages Matt to leave him, but Matt refuses to leave his friend. Matt tries to stay awake by telling Israel about the future. When Matt finally dozes off, Mr. Hornbee, a local farmer, wakes Matt and takes him away to the relative safety of his farm. Though the Hornbees are patriots, Mrs. Hornbee won't risk sheltering Matt. Mr. Hornbee sends Matt to the river on his mule Blackjack.

| Vocabulary |
| --- |
| violently |
| phlegm |
| spasms |
| agony |
| brusque |
| enticing |
| encased |
| wriggling |
| savoring |
| garment |
| drab |
| militia |
| jittery |
| clearance |
| plundering |
| yonder |
| profound |

## Discussion Questions

1. Matt feels responsible for Katie's safety. He also refuses to leave Israel. What do these things tell you about Matt? (*Answers will vary. Suggestions: Matt is a leader. He takes responsibility for others' care.*)

2. Why does Henry tell Matt it is better to leave Israel? What would you have done? (*Henry means that it is better for Matt to let Israel go than drag him further. Staying with Israel also means Matt risks dying too; Answers will vary.*)

3. Matt promises Israel that he will get the beads to Abby. How do you think Matt intends to keep this promise? (*Answers will vary.*)

4. Why does Mr. Hornbee insist on hurrying to his farm? (*If any of the Tories living in the area tell Colonel Rall the patriots are down the road, the colonel will send Hessians and rebel hunters. Mr. Hornbee wants to be safely home.*)

5. Why is Mrs. Hornbee afraid? Do you think her fear is reasonable, or should Matt's welfare be more important? (*Mr. Hornbee is a patriot, so he refused to sign the King's protection papers; his farm is not safe from British and Hessian troops. The Hornbees could lose everything, including their lives. Answers will vary.*)

6. How does Mr. Hornbee react when Matt says he is from the twentieth century? What is Mrs. Hornbee's reaction? (*Mr. Hornbee doesn't believe Matt and asks if Matt has recently received a wound to the head. Mrs. Hornbee says Matt must leave at once.*)

7. Why do you think Mr. Hornbee says, "Don't you think too badly of us, Matthew" (p. 95)? What is your opinion of the Hornbees? (*Answers will vary. Suggestions: Mr. Hornbee is probably ashamed of sending Matt away. The Hornbees are good people, but they are afraid.*)

8. **Prediction:** What will happen when Matt meets the Indians?

## Supplementary Activities

1. Speaking: Organize a classroom debate. Half of the class should prepare arguments supporting the position of the Patriots. The other half should prepare arguments supporting the position of the Loyalists. Also discuss possible solutions to each side's differences that would avoid war.

2. Critical Thinking: Mrs. Hornbee reminds Matt of Mrs. Pritchet, his second-grade teacher. Choose a character from the novel that reminds you of someone you know. Explain your choice in a short essay.

3. Social Studies: The zipper on Matt's jeans puzzles Mr. Hornbee. Research the history of the zipper. Share your findings with the class in an oral report.

4. Creative Writing: Write a story about what Mr. Hornbee does with Matt's sneaker. Be creative!

5. Social Studies: Matt enjoys seeing America before highways and shopping centers. Research the area where you live. Look for pictures and descriptions from the past. Present your findings to the class on a poster.

## Chapters Sixteen–Eighteen

Two Indian boys frighten Matt until he realizes Tony and Hooter are with them. Tony explains that before Adam Hibbs died he said the rowboat could take them home. Tony also tells Matt the Hessians have Q and Katie. When Tony and Hooter doubt his leadership skills, Matt remembers the impossible odds Washington faced and the general's courage. Matt knows he, too, must show courage. In exchange for a video game and shoe buckles, the Indians guide Matt, Tony, and Hoot to where the Hessians are holding Katie and Q and then disappear into the woods. Matt convinces Tony and Hooter to fight the Hessians.

| Vocabulary |
| --- |
| embraced |
| calf |
| resumed |
| implored |
| crucial |
| terrain |
| gait |
| forging |
| warrior |
| ruddy |
| ambush |
| surrender |

### Discussion Questions

1. Why does Matt feel weak, soft, and frightened even when he sees the Indians are boys? What do you think is the difference between the Indians and Matt? (*The Indians display fierceness, courage, and strength that Matt has never seen in boys before. Answers will vary but should include that the Indian boys know how to survive in the wild, while Matt is used to the comforts of modern living.*)

2. If Adam Hibbs had lived, do you think he would have wanted to travel through time with the Adventure Club or just help them return home? (*Answers will vary.*)

3. What is Q's plan? Where did he get this idea? (*to follow the soldiers to Matt and then return to the rowboat, which will take them home; Before Adam Hibbs died, Q is sure Adam said the boat would take them back home.*)

4. Why can't Hooter and Tony look Matt in the eyes? What do you think Matt would have done in their situation? (*They're embarrassed that they didn't try to stop the Hessians when they took Q and Katie and stopped to rest instead of following. Answers will vary.*)

5. Why don't the Indians understand Matt when he imitates Katie by crawling around with his thumb in his mouth, yet they understand when he uses berries to indicate Katie's red hair? (*Answers will vary, but should include that the Indians do not need silly gestures to convey ideas. Rather, using specific symbols, like the color red, helps them understand that Matt is talking about Katie, who has red hair.*)

6. Compare and contrast Tony and Hooter's opinions of Matt's leadership. Which character acts most like you would? (*Hooter is positive and trusts Matt to get them home. Tony expresses his doubts and blames Matt for the situation. Answers will vary.*)

7. Summarize what Matt has learned about impossible situations, courage, and himself. (*Matt takes responsibility for members of the Adventure Club and the situation they are in. Although he is afraid, has doubts, and doesn't have all the answers, he realizes he has courage and has held up pretty well facing dangers. Like Washington, Matt is willing to keep going.*)

8. How are the Hessian soldiers different from Matt's expectations? Why does he still consider them a formidable foe? (*The Hessians aren't "bloodthirsty giants" but regular men with tall hats and impressive uniforms. Matt knows the Hessians are well-trained, professional soldiers.*)

9. Q seems to be making friends with the Hessians until they find his dollar bill. Do you think Q could have resolved the situation if Matt, Tony, and Hooter hadn't been there? (*Answers will vary.*)

10. **Prediction:** What will happen when the Adventure Club fights the Hessians?

## Supplementary Activities

1. Social Studies: Research the role of American Indians in the Revolutionary War. Imagine that you are one of the Indian boys with Matt and his friends. Decide whether you would help the American or British army. Explain your choice in an essay.

2. Drama: Working with a partner, create a skit about an Indian boy who teaches Matt how to survive in the woods.

3. History: Most of Washington's troops were not well-trained, professional soldiers. Research how a man named Baron Friedrich Wilhelm Augustus von Steuben trained American soldiers at Valley Forge. Discuss Steuben's training methods in class.

4. Art: Create the comic strip that made the Hessian officer smile. Don't forget that the officer does not understand English. Your comic may include captions, but the meaning must be shown in the pictures.

# Chapters Nineteen–Twenty

Matt, Hooter, and Tony reach for the Hessians' rifles but surrender when the soldiers draw their swords. One of the soldiers, Gustav, marches the Adventure Club toward his camp. At the river, Katie falls through the ice, and Gustav rescues her. Moments later, Gustav is shot and killed by rebel soldiers. Matt is sick when the rebels make fun of the dead Hessian; he'd always dreamed of the rebel soldiers as honorable and brave men. Matt sees a soldier with Israel's beads. Washington arrives, tired but victorious, and gives Katie his extra pair of socks because she is wet. Washington promises Matt that he will make sure Israel's sister receives the beads. As the children say goodbye to Gustav's body, they realize that both armies have "good and bad" soldiers and that war is horrible.

| Vocabulary |
| --- |
| buck |
| severest |
| intent |
| diverted |
| slain |
| frisk |
| turncoats |
| stout |
| victorious |
| despite |
| vague |
| awestruck |
| solemnly |

## Discussion Questions

1. How does Tony's attitude affect Katie? (*Answers will vary but should include that Tony is being negative and talking about dying, which frightens Katie, making her ask for her mom.*)

2. The Adventure Club doesn't know how to control the time-traveling rowboat. Do you think Matt and his friends should stay where they are or try to go home and risk finding themselves in a worse situation? (*Answers will vary.*)

3. Why are the Hessians fighting in a war they "don't know anything about" (p. 131)? (*King George is running out of British soldiers so he hires the Hessians.*)

4. Why is Matt annoyed with Hooter? Do you agree with Matt? (*Hooter is friendly to Gustav, and Matt considers Gustav the enemy. Answers will vary.*)

5. What is the bravest thing Matt has ever seen anyone do? Why does this make him feel guilty? (*Gustav rescuing Katie on the ice; Matt is too embarrassed to thank Gustav because he feels bad about considering Gustav the enemy.*)

6. What upsets Matt about the way the rebels treat Gustav's body? (*Matt considers the soldiers "his rebels" and "special brave men." Seeing the soldiers behaving badly, treating Gustav as if he weren't a person, makes Matt realize the soldiers aren't the soldiers in his dreams.*)

7. What are George Washington's feelings about the war? (*Washington is deeply saddened that so many have lost their lives, yet he feels obligated to lead the soldiers as they fight for freedom.*)

8. How is war in real life different from war on TV? What does Matt mean when he says, "I thought this was supposed to be one of the good wars" (p. 144)? (*In real life, there are good and bad soldiers on both sides; on TV, the good guys and bad guys are easy to tell apart. Matt thought the rebels were good guys, fighting for the right reasons, but after meeting soldiers from both sides, he realizes that there is good and bad on both sides and that sometimes they're fighting for the same things.*)

9. **Prediction:** Will the Adventure Club return to the twentieth century?

## Supplementary Activities

1. Art: Research the history of Band-Aids®. Illustrate your findings.

2. Speaking: Research one of the following topics about Hessian soldiers: (1) the tall brass mitre caps worn by the Hessian Grenadiers, (2) Hessian soldiers who remained in America after the war. Share your findings in class.

3. Art: Paul Revere and Benjamin Franklin both engraved Continental currency. Design a dollar bill that represents the Revolutionary War.

4. Comprehension: Matt says that Israel and Gustav are not that different except for their uniforms. Use the Venn diagram on page 26 of this guide to compare and contrast Israel and Gustav.

## Chapters Twenty-one–Twenty-three

Katie earns membership in the Adventure Club when she takes the boys to the rowboat. The boys, seeing a reflection of the inscription "Emit Levart," realize it spells "time travel" backwards. As they debate how to activate the boat, Katie climbs in and says she wants to go home. The boat trembles, and the boys quickly board. Once home, everyone promises to keep the adventure a secret. They hide the boat for future adventures along with Washington's socks and Mrs. Hornbee's shoes. Q insists that Washington's socks not be left in the boat, but kept in a place of reverence, such as his private museum. Katie trades the socks to Q for a bag of marshmallows. The Adventure Club members are glad to be back home; though they liked the adventure, they know they belong in their own time. Matt and Katie's parents assume the kids used their imaginations when Katie can't keep a secret and talks about being with George Washington and his troops. Matt's dad says how proud he is of Matt for including Katie, that Matt is becoming a mature and responsible person. The story ends as Matt's father reaches for the sugar bowl, which still contains Matt's peas.

| Vocabulary |
| --- |
| dispel |
| anxiety |
| console |
| activate |
| encircled |
| depart |
| unruly |
| unraveled |
| chorus |
| utmost |
| antique |
| lush |
| divulge |

**Discussion Questions**

1. What is the importance of "Emit Levart"? Did you solve this before the solution was given? (*Emit Levart spelled backwards is "time travel"; Answers will vary.*)

2. What is the meaning of "the victory at Trenton had been long in coming" (p. 152)? (*Answers will vary. Suggestions: The Continental Army had been losing battles, especially in New York, and had retreated to New Jersey. The victory at Trenton was a turning point in the war.*)

3. How does Matt know they are no longer on the Delaware River? (*The water is warm; Matt finds a potato chip bag in the lake; he can see Tony's house.*)

4. What has Q read about time travel? Why does this make Matt happy? (*A person time traveling may be gone for a long time but return to find only a few hours have passed. Matt hopes their parents don't know they were gone.*)

5. Tony says if he told his father he'd spent the night with George Washington that his father would "probably make him go to therapy or something" (p. 157). Can you think of a way Tony could convince his father he is telling the truth? (*Answers will vary. Suggestions: Tony could show his father George Washington's socks, Mrs. Hornbee's shoes, and the rowboat.*)

6. Why does Q believe he can keep Washington's socks safely hidden? What would you do with them? (*Q collects so many things that scare his mother, including bones and mice, Matt is sure his mother won't come into his room or notice the socks. Answers will vary.*)

7. **Prediction:** Where will the Adventure Club's next adventure take place?

## Supplementary Activities

1. Comprehension: The Adventure Club learns "thoughts have something to do with the power of the boat" (p. 154). As a class, discuss problems that might happen if time travel depended on thoughts (e.g., being in the right place but in the wrong year; wanting to go someplace where there isn't a lake, ocean, or river). With a partner, create a manual about how to use the time travel boat.

2. Writing: Write a paragraph explaining how the story would be different if Tony, Hooter, or Q were president of the Adventure Club.

3. Critical Thinking: Choose a time in history that you would like to visit. List what you would like about that time and what you would miss from home. Consider how your lists would change if you time traveled to a place in the future.

4. Comprehension: A fact is information that can be proven. An opinion is a personal viewpoint. Find five facts and five opinions in the novel. Share your findings with the class.

# Post-reading Discussion Questions

1. What did you learn from reading George Washington's Socks? Do you think the author portrayed history accurately? (*Answers will vary.*)

2. Has reading the novel changed how you think about George Washington? How does the novel compare to other books you have read about Washington? (*Answers will vary. Discussion topics: why Washington is considered a great man and "Father of Our Country"*)

3. Imagine Matt convinces George Washington that he truly is from the future. How might Washington act differently? How would this change the story in George Washington's Socks? (*Answers will vary. Discussion Topics: the questions Washington would ask Matt about the upcoming battle, the war, and the future of America; how knowing the future might affect Washington's actions and battle plans*)

4. The picture on the novel cover is based on a famous painting called *Washington Crossing the Delaware*. Examine the picture. Do you see any historical inaccuracies? (*Answers will vary. Suggestions: The flag and the type of boats are wrong. Washington is standing, which would result in falling overboard like Katie did. See Background Information on page 3 of this guide.*)

5. Read "About the Author" at the back of the novel. What is a pacifist? Do you think the author is still a pacifist after researching and writing George Washington's Socks? (*someone who believes war is an unacceptable way of solving disputes; Answers will vary.*)

6. What scene in the novel is your favorite? Why? (*Answers will vary.*)

7. What are the messages in the novel? Explain which one you think is most important and why. (*Answers will vary.*)

8. What important lesson does Matt learn about leadership? Do you think he is a good leader? (*A person can be afraid but still be courageous and overcome obstacles, etc. Answers will vary.*)

9. What two promises does Matt keep in the story? How important do you think it is to keep promises? (*getting the beads to Abby, getting the members of the Adventure Club home safely; Answers will vary.*)

10. Would you like to read another story about the Adventure Club? Why or why not? (*Answers will vary.*)

# Post-reading Extension Activities

## Writing

1. Imagine that Matt finds the rowboat while he and Israel are marching toward Trenton. Write a story about Matt taking Israel to present-day Nebraska.

2. The Adventure Club leaves sneakers, a Band-Aid, and a video game in 1776. Write a story about the Adventure Club discovering how these items changed history.

3. Create a newspaper from 1776. Write an article that reports on the Continental Army crossing the Delaware River and the Battle of Trenton. Report opinions on these events in a "Letters to the Editor" section. Include letters from Patriots, Loyalists, Indians, and American, British, and Hessian soldiers.

## Speaking

4. Recite a speech or poem about freedom. It may be written by you or someone else.

5. Research George Washington's connection to the United States Military Academy at West Point, New York. Lead a class discussion based on your findings.

6. Work with a partner and research the causes of the American Revolution. Lead a class debate where one partner argues for the British and the other partner argues for the American rebels. Was the war justified or could another solution have been found?

## Art

7. Cut squares from colored construction paper (or fabric). Write the following information from *George Washington's Socks* on your cutouts: title, author, characters (one per square), settings, themes, and story summary. Use a different color for each topic (e.g., red for characters, blue for themes). Include squares with illustrated scenes from the novel. Assemble your quilt, and display in class.

8. Review the predictions you made while reading the novel. Choose one of your incorrect predictions. Illustrate how the novel would have been different if your prediction had come true. Include captions that explain the changes.

9. Make a model that shows your feelings about patriotism and America.

## Drama/Music

10. Working with your class, create a play about *George Washington's Socks*. Perform your play for students in younger grades.

11. Compose a song about George Washington. Put your lyrics to the tune of one of your favorite songs.

12. With three other partners, create a comedic skit about a scene in *George Washington's Socks* and perform the skit for the class in person or record your skit on video.

## Social Studies

13. Prepare an illustrated time line highlighting important events in the Revolutionary War.

14. Research Revolutionary War flags. Illustrate one flag, and write a caption for your artwork.

15. Write a report, complete with a poster or illustrations, about the submarine *Turtle* and its 1776 appearance in the Revolutionary War.

16. Organize a museum exhibit about the Revolutionary War. Have classmates create written information and photo displays. Include music and recipes. Appoint curators to answer questions. Curators should wear Revolutionary War costumes and wigs. Then invite other classes to visit your museum.

17. Research the effects of the Revolutionary War on American life and present a written historical alternative discussing what might have happened if the British had won the war. How would America have been different immediately after the war? How would it be different 200 years later?

# Assessment for *George Washington's Socks*

Assessment is an ongoing process. The following ten items can be completed during the novel study. Once finished, the student and teacher will check the work. Points may be added to indicate the level of understanding.

Name _____ Date _____

**Student**      **Teacher**

_____      _____      1. Complete the activities from the Revolutionary War Concept Map on page 23 of this guide.

_____      _____      2. Discuss your KWL chart in class. Summarize what you have learned about George Washington from reading the novel.

_____      _____      3. Read the letter George Washington sent to the Continental Congress describing the victory at Trenton, New Jersey. The letter is dated December 27, 1776, and can be found at the Library of Congress Web site (http://memory.loc.gov/learn/features/timeline/amrev/ north/trenton.html [active at time of publication]). In a short essay, compare the details in the letter with those found in *George Washington's Socks*.

_____      _____      4. Choose a word, sentence, paragraph, or scene that you think best shows the author's purpose for writing *George Washington's Socks*. Write a short essay explaining your choice.

_____      _____      5. Complete the Understanding Values chart on page 27 of this guide.

_____      _____      6. Complete the Cause and Effect Map on page 28 of this guide.

_____      _____      7. Complete the Effects of Reading chart on page 29 of this guide.

_____      _____      8. Write an essay on how traveling back to 1776 affects Matt's opinion of the courage of Revolutionary War soldiers. Use examples from the book to support your ideas.

_____      _____      9. Write a review of the novel. Include whether you would recommend the book to other readers. Explain why.

_____      _____      10. Create a booklet about five historical places the Adventure Club could time travel to next. Include illustrations of your choices. Name the people Matt and his friends might meet and what items they could bring back.

# KWL

**Directions:** As the book or content area is studied, fill in this chart. Before reading, review what you KNOW (about the setting and background) in the **K** column. The **W** column is for questions for which you WANT to find answers. The **L** column is completed after reading to list what you have LEARNED.

| K | W | L |
|---|---|---|
|   |   |   |

# Revolutionary War Concept Map

**Directions:** Complete the activity described in each of the boxes below.

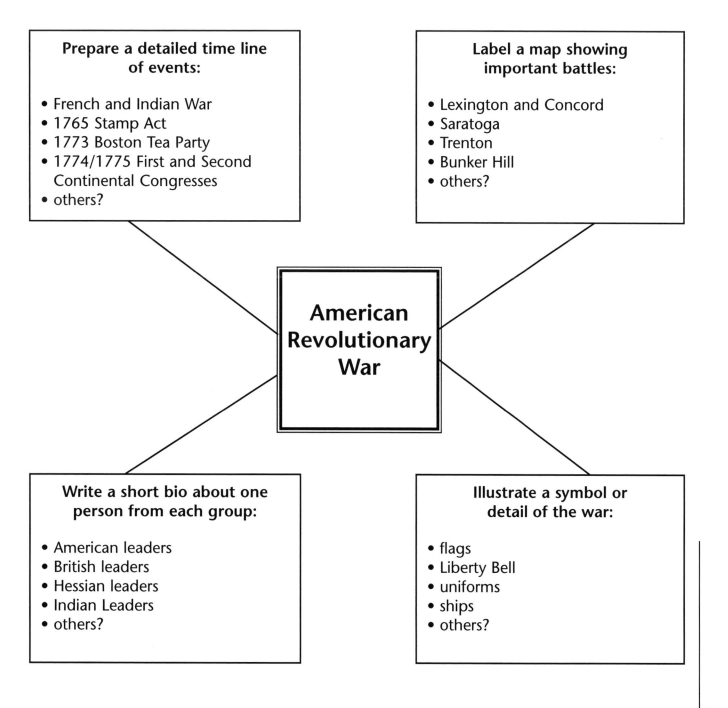

**Prepare a detailed time line of events:**

- French and Indian War
- 1765 Stamp Act
- 1773 Boston Tea Party
- 1774/1775 First and Second Continental Congresses
- others?

**Label a map showing important battles:**

- Lexington and Concord
- Saratoga
- Trenton
- Bunker Hill
- others?

**American Revolutionary War**

**Write a short bio about one person from each group:**

- American leaders
- British leaders
- Hessian leaders
- Indian Leaders
- others?

**Illustrate a symbol or detail of the war:**

- flags
- Liberty Bell
- uniforms
- ships
- others?

# Prediction Chart

| What characters have we met so far? | What is the conflict in the story? | What are your predictions? | Why did you make these predictions? |
| --- | --- | --- | --- |
| | | | |

# Story Map

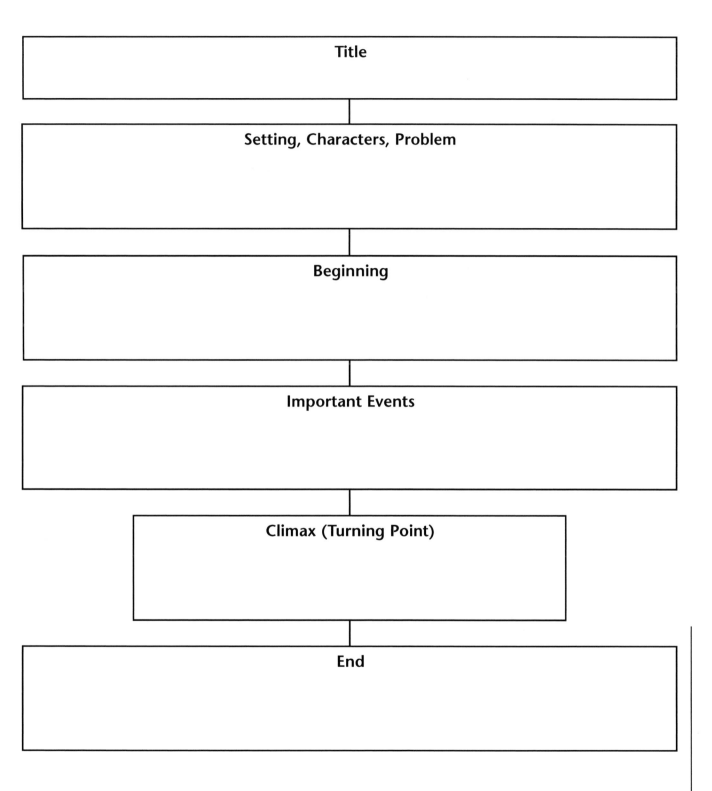

**Title**

**Setting, Characters, Problem**

**Beginning**

**Important Events**

**Climax (Turning Point)**

**End**

# Venn Diagram

**Directions:** Use the graphic below to compare and contrast Israel and Gustav.

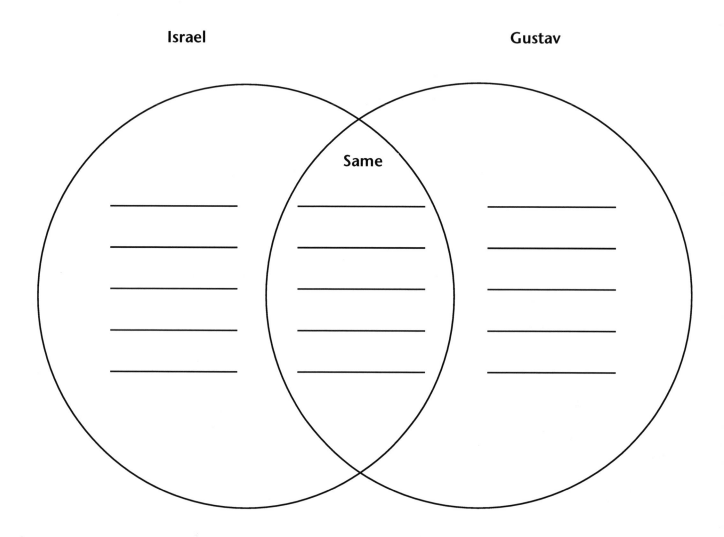

Israel

Gustav

Same

# Understanding Values

**Values** represent people's beliefs about what is important, good, or worthwhile. For example, most families value spending time together.

**Directions:** Think about the following characters from the novel and the values they exhibit. What do they value? What beliefs do they have about what is important, good, or worthwhile? On the chart below, list each character's three most important values, from most important to least. Be prepared to share your lists during a class discussion.

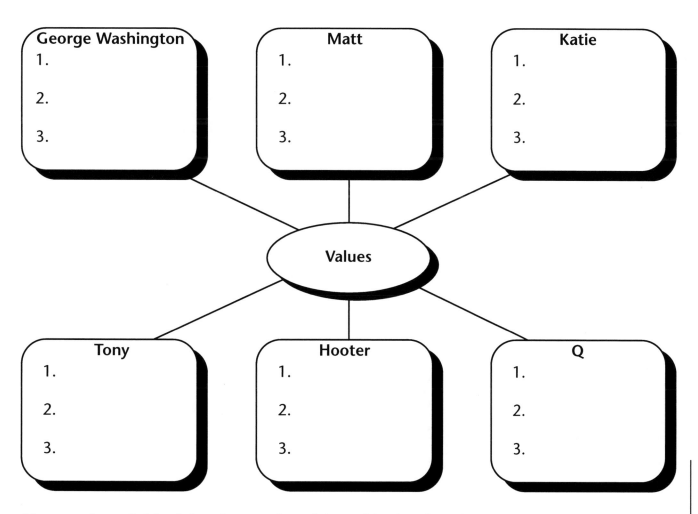

After you have finished the chart and participated in the class discussion, think about which character seems to have values most like your own. Write a paragraph that explains why you chose this character.

# Cause/Effect Map

**Directions:** List events that cause Matt to become a good leader. Write the events in the rectangles pointing to the effect.

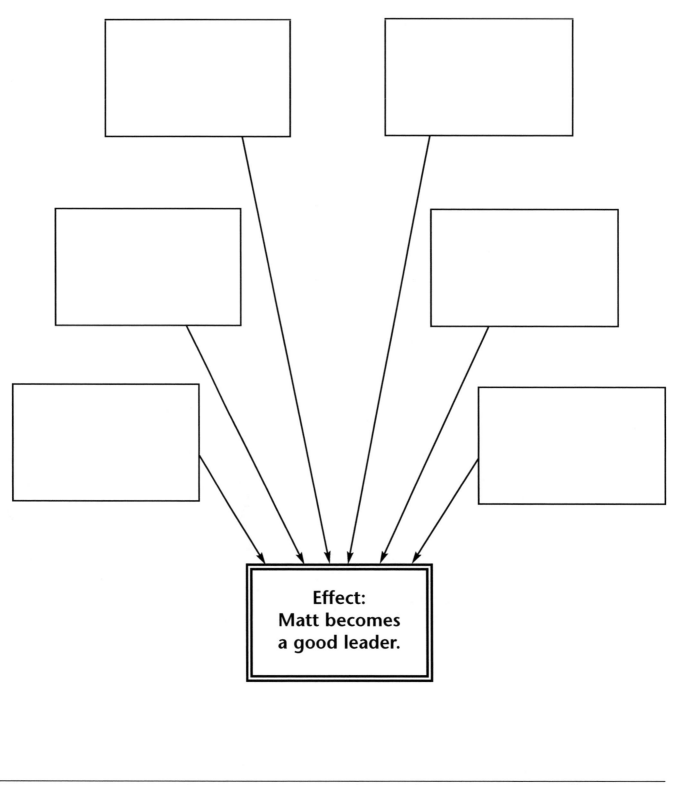

# Effects of Reading

**Directions:** When reading, each part of a book may affect you in a different way. Think about how *George Washington's Socks* affected you in different ways. Did some parts make you laugh? cry? want to do something to help someone? Below, list one part of the book that touched each of the following parts of the body: your head (made you think), your heart (made you feel), your funny bone (made you laugh), or your feet (spurred you to action).

| Your head | Your heart |
| --- | --- |
| | |

| Your funny bone | Your feet |
| --- | --- |
| | |

# Linking Novel Units® Lessons to National and State Reading Assessments

During the past several years, an increasing number of students have faced some form of state-mandated competency testing in reading. Many states now administer state-developed assessments to measure the skills and knowledge emphasized in their particular reading curriculum. The discussion questions and post-reading questions in this Novel Units® Teacher Guide make excellent open-ended comprehension questions and may be used throughout the daily lessons as practice activities. The rubric below provides important information for evaluating responses to open-ended comprehension questions. Teachers may also use scoring rubrics provided for their own state's competency test.

*Please note:* The Novel Units® Student Packet contains optional open-ended questions in a format similar to many national and state reading assessments.

## Scoring Rubric for Open-Ended Items

**3-Exemplary**
- Thorough, complete ideas/information
- Clear organization throughout
- Logical reasoning/conclusions
- Thorough understanding of reading task
- Accurate, complete response

**2-Sufficient**
- Many relevant ideas/pieces of information
- Clear organization throughout most of response
- Minor problems in logical reasoning/conclusions
- General understanding of reading task
- Generally accurate and complete response

**1-Partially Sufficient**
- Minimally relevant ideas/information
- Obvious gaps in organization
- Obvious problems in logical reasoning/conclusions
- Minimal understanding of reading task
- Inaccuracies/incomplete response

**0-Insufficient**
- Irrelevant ideas/information
- No coherent organization
- Major problems in logical reasoning/conclusions
- Little or no understanding of reading task
- Generally inaccurate/incomplete response

# Notes

# Notes